Anonymous

The World's Fairs

Anonymous

The World's Fairs

ISBN/EAN: 9783337817107

Printed in Europe, USA, Canada, Australia, Japan

Cover: Foto ©Thomas Meinert / pixelio.de

More available books at **www.hansebooks.com**

THE

WORLD'S FAIRS.

LETTERS ON INTERNATIONAL EXHIBITIONS

BY

A COMMISSIONNER TO VIENNA

IN 1873.

GENEVA, 1879.

BY THE SAME AUTHOR.

Die Amerikanischen National-Banken und die Deutsche Bankfrage.

[The American National Bank System and the German Bank Question].

FRIEDR. MAUKE. JENA, 1872.

Wanderversammlungen & Spezial-Ausstellungen.

[Nomadic Congresses and Special Exhibitions].

Separatabdrücke aus der Eichstädter Bienenzeitung, dem "Apicoltore", etc.

MILANO, 1876.

Grundzüge Deutscher Eisenbahnpolitik.

[Fundamental Principles of German Railway Policy].

KARL J. TRUBNER, STRASSBURG, 1877.

THE

WORLD'S FAIRS.

PRINTING OFFICE

OF THE

"CONTINENT AND SWISS TIMES"

GENEVA.

THE

WORLD'S FAIRS

LETTERS ON INTERNATIONAL EXHIBITIONS

By

A COMMISSIONNER TO VIENNA

In 1873.

GENEVA, 1879

REPRINTED FROM
THE CONTINENT AND SWISS TIMES.

CONTENTS.

I.

good order of working depen ls upon a common agreement between the nations. —Want of such an agreement in regard to Universal Exhibitions.—Both London and Paris desire to monopolise the exhibition idea.— Other nations defend their economical independance.—As Universal Exhibitions become frequent, « the interest of trade » must be their ruling principle.--The international comparison and judgement of products become, on the other hand, the ruling principle of

IV.

Internal organization of exhibitions.— The Administration of an exhibition should unite commercial simplicity and expedition with bureaucratical conscientiousness. — International dissatisfaction, the result of a one-sided distribution of the exhibiting room.— Baron Schwartz and the German Commission.— Error of the German Commission in making uniformity, instead of diversity, the aim of their national exhibition policy. — Misplaced application of the principle of centralisation. --The duties of an exhibition commission towards the State, the exhibitors and the public.—International courtesy and the civilising influence of exhibi-

THE WORLD'S FAIRS.

I.

The International Exhibition at Paris has hardly closed, and already we hear of a project to organise a new one at New York. Those countries, which have as yet not had their own great international exhibitions, particularly Germany and Italy, are in all probability likewise maturing their plans at the present time. The moment is therefore well chosen for a retrospective glance at the salient features of our past exhibition experience.

It is the opinion of many, that international exhibitions, or as they may be more appropriately termed to distinguish them from special exhibitions, *Universal Exhibitions*, are becoming too frequent. A lapse of ten years has been very generally considered necessary, in order to allow of such improvements and new inventions being made, as to render a fresh comparative exhibition of them of real advantage. Within the last twelve years we have, however, had the four great exhibitions of Paris 1867, Vienna 1873, Philadelphia 1876, and now again Paris 1878, and the series promises to continue at the same rate.

The organisers of these exhibitions have evidently other aims, besides those truly cosmopolitan ones, which animated Prince Albert in organising the first great exhibition of London in 1851. In short, the international purpose has become more or less subservient to national interests, which are in part of the political, in part of the economical order. The periodical inspection of universal production in view of determining an epoch, in the development of human intelligence as a whole, is still outwardly maintained as the characterising quality of the undertaking, but it is no longer the essential purpose. This has in reality become a national one.

Thus the main object of the Vienna exhibition was to give new impulse to Austria's trade with the East, and to increase Vienna's importance as a centre of exchange for the trade between the eastern and western nations. In Philadelphia the leading idea was to give the American people themselves a vivid and striking picture of the prosperity and development attained by the United States in the century of their existence as a nation. The object this year in Paris was to convince the people of France, that the present republican form of government is as favorable to the prosperity of manufactures and commerce, as was the empire of Napoleon III.

If therefore the true cause of the exhibition is, as we see in these cases, the desire to obtain some definite political or economical advantage for the country, which has the exhibition, we must not be surprised to see the matter treated entirely as an act of inner politics, and consequently without any preliminary understanding with other nations. These are simply notified, that an international exhibition will be held at such a time and place, and they are invited to contribute to its success by sending their products, and paying for their exhibition.

Foreign countries are certainly then free to refuse their participation, but the nature of international exhibitions is such, that they cannot do so without injuring their own interests.

Germany refused to take part in the Paris exhibition of this year, but at a late hour sent pictures for the art department,

in order to show that economical con-
siderations, and not a feeling of hostility
for the French people or their government,
were the motives of this decision.

The United States have sent very insufficient samples of their production to
all the last European exhibitions, and it
has been entirely impossible to form a
correct idea of the developement and
ressources of the country from their department.

Such abstinence or insufficient participation cannot fail to be injurious to the
economical interests of a country taken in
their totality. The liens of solidarity,
which connect the economical interests of
the world, are not loosened with impunity,
and it remains as true for a whole country
as for an individual, that he who lags
behind is soon set aside by a more active
competitor. Thus we find Germany
punished for her insufficient representation
at Philadelphia by the wholesale branding
of her production with the trade mark
"poor and cheap," or as it has latterly
been improved "poor and dear." Already
at Vienna in 1873 the want of a preliminary judicious selection of the articles
to be exhibited made itself felt in the
German department. It seemed as if it
had been thought necessary to prove

Germany's economical importance to the world by bringing a specimen of every single article, that was produced in the country, to exhibition. The result was, that the visitor felt, as if he were in an immense general store or warehouse, and the best of articles remained unnoticed in the general mass. Many manufacturers were naturally disheartened by this experience, particularly as exhibiting under German bureaucratical direction is far from pleasant for practical business men. Under these circumstances the German department at Philadelphia turned out, as was to be foreseen, a failure. The commissioners, who should have felt personally responsable for this state of things, because they had not succeeded in making a profitable use of the large means placed at their disposal, anticipated all reproach for themselves, by unduly qualifying the nature of their country's products as poor and cheap, and consequently unable to make a better appearance at an exhibition. The German professor, who as chief of his commission gave this oracular explanation of Germany's want of success at Philadelphia, deserved to have the freedom of the city of Manchester offered to him. His compatriots at home have, however, learnt, that exhibition matters are a science, which the English and French commissioners understand, but those persons, who have been selected to represent German interests, have yet to master.

Bureaucracy, however perfect in theory, in practice does not always succeed in putting the right man in the right place at the right time. The entire want of bureaucracy may, on the contrary, have a great deal to do with the unsatisfactory appearance of the American department at the European exhibitions.

Taking into consideration the loss of prestige Germany has suffered at the last exhibitions, and at the same time the immense affluence of Germans to these exhibitions, it is evident that the fashion and taste for foreign products must from day to day grow stronger in that country, unless something is done to reinstate home manufactures in the national favor. The best means to do so is by an international exhibition, which places the domestic manufacturer on a most favorable footing against his foreign competitor. The public can then fairly judge, where its interest is to encourage home production, and where it is to be supplied by foreign trade. As an international exhibition has thus become an economical necessity for the country, we shall probably soon hear of some project for Berlin.

After the recent complete success of the patriotic undertaking at Philadelphia, it may seem surprising to see a New York project brought forward so soon. The explanation lies in the fact, that at the Centennial the political character dominated, and the economical interests took a secondary place. The channels of trade are not to be turned aside at will, and made subservient to other interests. Trade and commerce must be considered as final objects in themselves, and international exhibitions, which are to be of real advantage to them, must be dominated by this principle. New York, not Philadelphia, is the commercial capital of Northern America, and its natural intermediary in the trade of the world. An international exhibition in New York would consequently have the interest of trade for its ruling principle. Its character would therefore essentially differ from that of the Centennial exhibition at Philadelphia. From the standpoint of the economist it would be more in accordance with the nature of the institution.

The only true ruling principle for universal exhibitions must be the interest of trade, if they are not to degenerate to mere curiosity shows and fairs.

For the purposes of study or education on the contrary it is undeniable, that special exhibitions have the advantage over universal exhibitions, as in concentrating the enterprise in a more limited field, they allow a greater degree of perfection to be attained.

II.

The Exhibitions of Philadelphia 1876 and of Paris 1878 were successful. The French anti-republican press, which styled the late Exhibition "le Bazar de Monsieur Krantz," did the undertaking little harm. Their weak attacks were less injurious than the general dissatisfaction, which prevailed among journalists at Vienna in 1873, and was caused by the establishment of an official exhibition press bureau, which monopolised exhibition news for a single paper. This unfavorable feeling of the press, the great commercial crash of the 1st of May 1873, and the visit of the cholera may well be considered the causes, which somewhat marred the success of the Vienna Exhibition.

If we judge the exhibitions by their plan of arrangement, the one of Paris 1867 has hardly been surpassed by the later ones. The main building had the form of an ellipsis and was divided into a number of annular galleries or zones, each of which was devoted to a particular group or class of goods, and thus formed a complete special exhibition in itself.

The departments of the different nations were divided off by radial or transversal galleries intersecting all the annular galleries. In following one of the radial galleries the visitor successively reviewed all the different products of the same country, while in passing through an annular gallery he was enabled to compare the same class of goods from all countries. It would also have been possible to make the annular galleries correspond to the different national departments, by proportioning their size to the importance of the country, and then to so arrange the goods, that the transversal galleries would always intersect the same class of goods.

The facility for comparative studies, and particularly for the work of the Jury, which similar systems of arrangement offer, are evident, and need no comment. They can of course be as easily adapted to buildings of angular form, as to those of circular form. And as the outward appearance can therefore be varied at will, it would perhaps have been advisable to have adopted such an arrangement once for all, at least for those classes of goods, which it is the object of the exhibition to bring into comparison.

Perfectly compatible with such arrangement of the main building are separate ex-

hibitions of ethnographical interest, or of
such products, which are monopolies, and
consequently have no competitors to be
compared to. At Vienna the different cot-
tages, and particularly the Alsatian farm,
which contained an exhibition of agricul-
tural and alimentary products, attracted
great attention. At Philadelphia the
buildings of the foreign commissions were
much admired. These separate buildings
ornament the exhibition grounds, they
vividly impress the imagination, and
agreeably vary the unavoidable monotony
of the general exhibition.

In trying to improve upon the idea,
it has been spoilt at the last Paris
exhibition. There dwelling houses of
different nations were set up side by
side in a long unbroken row, the so-
called street of nations, which was
in fact an inner, but uncovered gallery of
the exhibition. Instead of a series of separate pictures, each complete in itself,
the visitor here only took away with him
the remembrance of a confused mixture
of international façading.

It is a fact worth remarking, that
each of the three last universal exhibitions has endowed its city with a
lasting architectural monument, which
during the exhibition time represented, as
it were, the characteristic feature.

The immense Rotunda of Vienna, with a dome that equals that of St Peter's at Rome in size, now serves for concerts and popular festivals. During the exhibition the Rotunda contained a thoroughly international selection of the most valuable products from all the departments. This idea had the disadvantage of, as it were, discounting in advance the decisions of the Jury. To be in the Rotunda gave an exhibitor at once an advantage over his competitors. This can not have been the intention of the organising committee, who in thus forming a small universal exhibition within the large one, were probably mainly actuated by the wish to give the immense Rotunda some useful besides ornamental employment in connection with the exhibition. They would probably have better attained their end by making it, the department of plastic art, whose subjects would have presented a more harmonious aspect, than did the heterogenous mass of industrial products.

In beauty of the grounds the Philadelphia exhibition surpassed those of Europe; and Memorial Hall, which permanently adorns Fairmount Park, can rank worthily by the side of the Vienna Rotunda and the Trocadero Palace at Paris.

This fine building contained the art department of the exhibition, and it now continues in the same service as a museum. If the United States thus give the place of honor at home to art, they do not show the same attention for their art department in the European exhibitions. A popular French guide book to the Paris Exhibition (Gautier & Desprez, Paris 1878, vide p. 62) explained the fact, that there was little worth seeing in the American department, by the assertion "ce peuple n'est pas encore arrivé au sentiment de l'art!"

Instead of wasting words on a picture, which has no originality, and merely imitates a lower kind of parisian style—a vulgar female laughing over the "Journal pour rire,"—it would have been more just, if American Art was to be judged by the pictures exhibited, to draw public attention to Dana's "Solitude," representing the grand majesty of a high-going sea by moonlight, or to Bridgman's very original picture, "funeral scene in ancient Egypt."

If this guide book does not flatter American artists, it is certainly no less severe for the architects of the monumental building of the exhibition, the Trocadero Palace. It honestly states, that this building of arabesque style resembles

at the same time a church, the grand stand
of a race course and a railway station.

It is in truth, a motley mixture of different styles of architecture, but striking
in general appearance.

The name Trocadero is undoubtedly
derived from the Spanish word "trocar,"
to barter. It was very likely originally
given to the hill, on which the exhibition
building has been erected, in memory of
the taking of fort Trocadero on the island
of Léon, in front of Cadiz, by the French
expedition under the Duke of Angoulême,
sent to aid the Spanish Bourbons against
the insurgents in 1823. Perhaps this fort
had been built upon a site, which originally served for a place of barter, a
market or fair, and thus the etymological
meaning of the word renders its application to an exhibition building quite ap-
propriate.

The centre of the Trocadero palace is
occupied by an immense concert hall, "la
salle des fêtes," which holds 5000 persons,
and is probably the finest one in the
world.

The rest of the building, that is the
wings, was devoted to retrospective art.
A department we usually find in Museums
or in special exhibitions, such as the
art treasures exhibition at Manchester or

the one at Munich in 1876, but less frequently at universal exhibitions.

As Paris is in itself already a large industrial exposition, it was probably thought necessary to attract the general public to the exhibition, by giving Curiosities the prominent place. They were indeed the leading feature of this exhibition, both as regards the external appearance of the buildings and the objects exhibited. The Prince of Wales' Indian collection, the crown jewelry, &c. were the chief attractions in the main building, as were the antiquities in the Trocadero palace.

It would, however, be unfair not to state, that there were also collections of plain staple goods in the exhibition, which prove that the science of exhibiting is itself continually making progress. As an example we may well cite the collective exhibition of the Tanners of France. It occupied three large rooms in the main building, and may be considered a characteristic representation of the commercial honesty and solidity of French manufacturers. No sign of any "smart" attempt of an individual exhibitor to put himself unduly forward, and reap for himself the whole advantage of the common undertaking. A general goodwill of all the participants to do their very best in con-

cert, and gain credit for their trade as a
national one, appears in this exhibition, and
it therefore will certainly obtain an honor-
able place in the annals of exhibiting.

In France art and handicraft have
grown thoroughly together, and the spirit
of the fine arts pervades manufacturers.
Excellent training in the trades, social
consideration shown for both artisan and
artist, and general honest dealing have
given the French an undeniable su-
periority in many branches. Thus, for instance, in bronzes and in decorative art
generally, they are ahead of all other nations.

They are also thorough masters in the
art of favorably disposing their goods in
exhibitions, and showing them off to the
greatest advantage.

The engraved diplomas and the medals
of the Jury awards of the exhibition
of 1878, are well worth attention. The
former surpass all the previous ones in
artistic design. The latter, in antique
style, show on the face the head of the
French republic, on the obverse the god-
dess of fame, publishing to the world the
name of the successful exhibitor.

III.

The country, which is going to have an international exhibition, always loudly proclaims, that it is to be a festival of peace, an occasion of friendly unison for the nations of the world in a common enterprise, that is to benefit them all. Experience has proved, that no country can refuse its participation without doing injury to its own economical interests.

Now it has become an evident truth in our day, that liberty is the sine qua non condition of all progress in the domain of that science, which we call political or social economy. The innate power of the economical interests is such, that it has compelled all governments to unite in negotiations, in order to remove the restrictions on their freedom of action. It has at length come to be understood, that the means of communication, which are in the service of the economical interests must be treated as international property, and not from the standpoint of church steeple politics. Congresses, who meet to consider the nature of Railway, Post and Telegraph administrations, soon discover, that it needs nothing but common agreement, to establish that universal good order of working, which satisfies all interests.

In the subject which occupies our attention, we have an institution, which of all others belongs to this common domain. While this is admitted in theory, there is in practice, as much sharp play allowed rival national interests, as we can find in some petty trade competition, and mutual good will is at a premium.

Londoners would like to convince the world, that London is the only proper place for an international exhibition, as they consider their city the heart, as it were, of the commercial body of the world. Parisians oppose their own pretension, that Paris is the seat of its brain, and consequently has as good a right to come forward as London. Americans, Austrians, Germans, Italians and other nations are considered both by Londoners and Parisians in the light of tributaries only, who owe allegiance.

But the nations do not humbly submit to their self styled economical masters. Each one feeling, that it is in itself a complete economical organisation, is not willing to be made a secondary member of a collective organisation, of which another is to be the head. An international exhibition being one of the best means to stimulate the developement of the national ressources, and obtain the position, which is due in the community of nations, we find one country after another at work to organize its own world's fair.

What is the result? Manufacturers, finding it too expensive to be continually making preparations for exhibitions, frequently abstain from participating in them. The departments of the different nations consequently no longer offer a true picture of their economical developement. We find, that the nature of the institution itself changes, and its ruling principle must become, as has been indicated above, the interest of trade only.

No matter at what distant place a universal exhibition may be held, those who have interests there, who buy or sell in the country, are sure to take interest or to participate in it. It then becomes a field of competition, with

the home manufacturers on one side
and the foreign traders on the other.
The public, as supreme judge, examines
the pretensions of either party, and draws
the limits of their respective domain. The
ground plan of the last Paris exhibition,
showing the distribution of the different
departments, gives an illustration of this
fact. One half of the main building was
occupied by the French department and
the other half by the foreign exhibiters
collectively. It was more or less the
same at Philadelphia, and it will be in-
fallibly so at an exhibition in New York
or in Germany.

What becomes then of the original idea
of a public examination in the school of
nations, as it were, and of the rewarding
of the respective diligence by prizes? If
it is to be a serious one, and not to degenerate as it does in some schools, where
every child receives a prize, lest his
parents should become dissatisfied, and
take him away, this will have to become
the domain of *Special Exhibitions*, that is
Exhibitions especially organised for some
particular branch of manufactures, ma-
chinery for instance. The general plan of
such exhibitions, and the determination
of the epoch, at which they are to be
held, ought then, however, to be the

work of international agreement and
not the arbitrary decision of a single
nation.

These remarks do not of course apply
to works of art, an exhibition of which is
at all times to public advantage. The comparatively small cost of transport and
the high intrinsical value of sculptures
and paintings will always render it
profitable for their owners to exhibit them.
As an attraction for the general public,
they are a necessity for the pecuniary
success of all universal exhibitions.

Congresses, conferences and musical
entertainments are from this point of view
likewise excellent means of awakening
general interest, and bringing people into
town in exhibition times. We, however,
do not wish to insinuate by this remark,
that they do not also attain their special
ends, which are of a higher order.

IV.

After describing Universal Exhibitions
in some of their chief features, we have
shown, that their frequent repetition is
after all due to the influence of the economical interests. We have concluded
from this, that Universal Exhibitions
should be organised, when and where the
condition of manufactures and trade
demands them, but not as an instrument
of political demonstration.

As the exhibition countries now take
for themselves alone, one half of the exhibiting room, and leave only the other
half to the rest of the world collectively,
such exhibitions can no longer be considered the occasion of a thorough and
general comparison of the industrial
achievements of all nations. They must
in future be looked upon as the battlefield
of a country's domestic interests with the
interests of the commerce of the world.

We have in this an example of the apparent antagonism of interests, from which, however, finally results that harmony of interests, the existence of which political economists find so difficult to prove to the world.

It is evident, that a thorough and general comparison of the products of all nations and an infallible judgément of their respective merits by an international jury would require a previous common agreement, which the rivality of national interests renders almost impossible for an undertaking of such importance, as a Universal Exhibition. In the case of Special Exhibitions this agreement appears more easily attainable. There are so many different branches of manufactures, that it might be just possible to satisfy all parties by determining the order, in which international exhibitions of them, should be held, at least for the different central countries of Europe.

It now remains for us to examine the inner organization of Universal-Exhibitions. We do so by selecting, as an example, the exhibition of Vienna in 1873, for the foreign participation was more general there, than at the later exhibitions, and the policy of the German Commission to

that exhibition offers arguments in support of the general views, we wish to advance.

The Vienna exhibition was organised
by Baron Schwartz-Senborn, a man of
great power of imagination, whose mind
had fully grasped the idea of a truly universal exhibition, that would embrace
every field, on which human intellect has
been at work. Had his plan been entirely
successful both in its material and in its
ideal manifestation, it would have been a
perfect picture of all human science.

As it was, Baron Schwartz found great
difficulty in executing his plans. As
Director-General he honestly tried to place
himself above the standpoint of nationality,
and direct the participation of all nations
with the same impartiality. Admitting,
that he succeeded in doing so, his distribution of the departments or shares in the
exhibiting ground to the different nations
remained after all a one-sided decision,
based upon the personal conception, which
he had formed of the economical importance of the different countries. The German Empire for one, did not accept his
judgment of its economical position in the
world.

Thence sprang endless negotiations,
which kept the exhibitors in uncertainty

for months, and finally ended in an extension of the German department by means of vast annexes, which contributed little to the harmonious aspect and good arrangement of the whole exhibition.

If a country takes upon itself the guarantee of the immense expenses of an exhibition, it certainly has the right to determine the limits of the enterprise. It is also justified in reserving as much exhibiting room, as it pleases, for its own domestic products, but what may after that be placed at the disposal of foreign nations, ought, at least, to be divided among them upon the basis of a common agreement. Commissioners, who should not only be familiar with the commercial interests of their own country, but also with those of the country they are sent to, would not find it impossible to agree, particularly if they were all masters of the language of the country, as they ought to be. They would on their return home, moreover, all work in common accord in directing the participation of their respective countries, having from the very commencement been fully initiated into the views of the General Direction.

When the plan of the Vienna exhibition had been adopted, and foreign countries had declared their adhesion, Baron

Schwartz commenced to direct the work
of the commissions of the different countries, by the issue of special programmes
containing the leading ideas, and also regulations, for each group, or class of the
exhibition. It was an excellent thought,
but unfortunately many of these programmes appeared too late to be of much
use.

There always will be some dissatisfaction connected with international exhibitions. Their very nature, as a battlefield
of competing interests, implies this. Whole
nations will be disagreeably surprised to
find themselves distanced in the manufacture of some particular goods, in which
they believed to be masters. Individual
exhibitors will be annoyed at being clas-
sed after some more successful competitor,
in the decisions of the Jury.

Besides such unavoidable causes of dis-
pleasure, the defective or incomplete
training of the exhibition administration
gives rise to complaint.

The administration of any department
of the public service requires long years
to gradually attain a systematic and perfect working order. How much more difficult must it be, to create, spontaneously,
a reliable and intelligent service for an
undertaking, which has to be matured in

an exceedingly short space of time. The
last Exhibition at Paris, for instance, was
organised in only eighteen months.

It would be entirely impossible to attain
success without the help of an element already schooled in the public service.

Now, it is the fundamental principle of
all public service, that the employee has
conscientiously and obediently to carry out
the work, that is laid out for him, but not
to take any initiative upon himself. The
chief of the department alone bears the
responsability, and consequently not even
the most unimportant order can be exe-
cuted without his signature. If he had
nothing to do, but to sign orders, he
might get through with his work, but as
he is at the same time the moving spirit
of the entire department, he is always
overworked, and hardly ever able to be
fully "à jour."

In an exhibition administration this
will not do. Everything ought to be
settled at once, like the business of a commercial firm. From the very first determination of a certain date for the opening
of the exhibition, results that every con-
tract in connection with the exhibition is a
time-contract, the possibility of the exe-
cution of which depends upon an immediate decision.

The conditions vary with every day,
and if therefore the matter is left open or
unsettled for any length of time, endless
complications, law suits and other dis-
asters ensue. At Vienna, many tradesmen
found ruin, instead of profit, in contracting
for the exhibition, from this very reason.
Similar objections can be made to the
work of the Commissions. In federal
countries like the German Empire or the
United States, there is usually a Central
Commission named, with as many sub-
commissions, as there are sovereign
countries or states. As the General-
Direction of the exhibition reserves the
right of action on many questions of
detail, there is often a lengthy four-
handed correspondance going on between the exhibitor, the sub-commission,
the central-commission and the director-
general. In the official bureaux, letters
are usually copied by hand, and this becomes also one of the principal causes of
delay. Here at least the remedy would be
easy by means of a general introduction
of the copying-press.

It often takes months and months before
the exhibitor can obtain any decisive
answer, and as he is a business man, for
whom time is money, the delay not only
often doubles and trebles the expense of

the necessary preparations, but also takes
up more of his personal time and attention, than he can well afford. It is therefore not surprising, that leading manufacturers, who have an assured custom,
often refuse to participate in exhibitions.
It would be easy for any person acquainted
with the manufacturing interest in different countries, to cite examples from the
late exhibitions which show, that many
leading branches of trade were represented
exclusively by beginners, who have yet
their reputation to establish, but not by
houses of note.

Such was chiefly the cause of the unsatisfactory appearance of the German department at Philadelphia, but if a severe
criticism of it was therefore justified, yet,
the hasty deduction, that all German
manufactures were inferior, was wholly
unfounded.

We are of the opinion that the fault
lies in such cases much less on the side of
the manufacturers, than in the nature of
the administrations connected with the
exhibition. The problem here is, how to
unite commercial simplicity and expedition with bureaucratical conscientiousness ? It cannot be solved by abandon-
ing the direction to merchants, who are in
active business, and who have con-

sequently to take care of their own interests above everything else. The only
correct way is to adapt the commercial
system, which gives every department a
certain autonomy, to the reliable work of
conscientious officers of the Government.

The Vienna Exhibition, coming so soon
after the reunion of Germany, it was a
natural and laudable desire in those who
directed the participation of that country,
to endeavour to make its department a
faithful representation of the homogeneity
and strength of the new Empire. It was
their intention to show that the coronation
of the Emperor William I. had put an end
to the dissensions which made Germany
weak, and that, in future, her national interests, whether they be of a political or
an economical nature, are backed by the
united strength of one of the most power-
ful nations of the world.

The Commission sought to attain this
aim, by not only carefully effacing every
sign of the federal nature of the country,
but also by giving the arrangement of
their department and the outward appearance of the annexes they had built
at the Exhibition, the greatest uniformity
possible. For this reason also, the show-
cases and stands were, with few excep-
tions, all ordered from a single large con-

tractor, instead of being distributed, as an encouragement, to the trade in general.

The plans that were adopted left but little room for the exercise of the inventive ingenuity of the individual exhibitors in the arrangement of their goods. The interests, most directly concerned, were, therefore, made secondary to the above-mentioned patriotic purpose, and the chief attraction of exhibitions, diversity, was almost sacrificed in the German department to the contrary principle, uniformity.

Many persons who, like the writer, are declared partisans of centralisation, when applied to the means of communication, the arteries of trade, consider it a serious mistake whenever that principle is allowed to encroach directly on the domain of commerce and industry. We, therefore, consider it a mistaken conception of the duties of an Exhibition Commission, when they determine the dress, as it were, in which the national products are to present themselves. The manufacturer himself knows best which is the most advantageous manner of displaying his goods.

The Commission, as the intermediary between the General Direction and the exhibitors, should give every possible latitude to individual initiative, and not try to force it into a straight jacket, by

imposing their own ideas of taste and
beauty. It is the greatest advantage of
exhibitions, to give new impulse to the inventive ingenuity of the individual, and it
is by the arrangement, quite as much as
by the manufacture of the goods, that this
is done.

No one will deny that it is a great deal
easier for a Commission to impose their
own plan in detail, than to find an harmonious and attractive arrangement for the
varied results of individual taste. The
result is, however, not the same; the latter
renders the exhibition interesting, as every
detail is an original and complete conception in itself, while the former makes
what should only be the means, the chief
end.

To arrange their department satisfact-
orily, seems unfortunately always to have
been the great difficulty of the German
Commission at Universal Exhibitions. Thus
in the "Letters on England," by Louis
Blanc [English translation, 1866, Vol. II.,
page 61], we find the following criticism
of the German department at the London
International Exhibition of 1862 :

" We are assured that the Zollverein has
treasures to show, but, unfortunately, it
has not yet shown anything, through defective arrangement. What is seen, is

what might have been hidden, and what is hidden ought to have been brought into sight."

In a former article, we mentioned the collective exhibition of a French trade at this year's Exhibition in Paris. In such collective exhibitions of particular trades, Germany also obtained success at Vienna, and thus proved, if such proof was necessary after her many successful national exhibitions, that want of taste in arranging is not a national defect. As a Vienna example, we may cite the exhibition of the silk-makers of Crefeld, which was very fine indeed. The collections exhibited by the manufacturing chemists of Germany, were also very complete, they showed products second to none in fineness and purity of quality. These collective exhibitions have the advantage of bringing forward simultaneously a whole series of similar products. They economise room, and assure harmonious display as well as methodical arrangement.

It is the desire of the central authorities of the Empire at Berlin to encourage the legitimate independence of provincial developement in the domain of industrial enterprise. They wish to avoid the faults of the French imperial policy, which tried, on the contrary, to stifle the spirit of industrial and commercial progress, peculiar to each section of the country, and to force the life of the provinces into the Parisian model.

It is impossible, and if it were possible, it would not be desirable, for a nation of 42 millions of souls, which unites many different peoples with their own peculiar habits, tastes and ways of thinking, to attain excellence in taste, fashion and art, by giving these a single, so-called national, direction. Success can here only be obtained by carefully developing everything that is original or peculiar to any part of the country. Diversity is, after all, the attraction of life, and particularity should therefore be respected, as much as possible, both in the individual and in the race. A contrary policy can only advance those pernicious theories which preach death to individual liberty and developement, and finally arm, as we have lately seen, the hand of the assassin against the sacred representatives of civilised society.

If the principle of centralisation were to be made the basis of our entire social life, one might as well also decree, that only one particular dialect of a language be correct, and that the use of any other would be punished as a misdemeanour.

No doubt there are pedants enough who would like to see such a decree really passed. To us, a good broad dialect always sounds like the familiar voice of some old family friend, whom we feel pleasure in meeting after long years of absence. And we have a similar feeling, when we see at an exhibition the well-known products for which some locality is famous, appear in their particular national character.

The chief duty of an Exhibition Commission consists in seeing, that the capital, which is severally contributed to the undertaking by the State, the Exhibitors and the Public, be employed to the greatest advantage, and not rendered unproductive.

When the funds of the State are applied to encourage the participation of exhibitors, by contributing towards their expenses, this confers the right to make the permission to exhibit dependent upon the fulfilment of certain conditions, as to the quality and quantity of the goods to be exhibited. The more rigorous these conditions are made, the higher will be the value attached to exhibiting, and the greater the effort to excel.

It is comparatively easy to ascertain what particular classes of goods are likely

to find a market in the country of the
exhibition, and it should be a peculiar
aim of the Commissioners to encourage
the manufacturers of such goods to
exhibit.

It is for the Commission to watch that
neither the general interests of the nation
be sacrificed to the individual interests
of the exhibitors, nor the reverse. Exhibitors will best serve both their own and
the national interests, by sending goods
of current manufacture and sale, but of
careful workmanship, and which are
marked with the common price of sale at
the place of manufacture. Even the most
successful exhibitors find, however, that
the advantages to be obtained by an Exhibition in increase of business rarely appear at once, but require two or three
years to gradually establish themselves.

It has long been the usage at Agricul-
tural Shows and other Special Exhibitions
to give exhibitors immediate encouragement by buying up their goods for a lottery, to be held at the closing of the exhibition. At Paris this has now been tried
for the first time at a Universal Exhibition; should the attempt prove satisfactory,
judicious lottery purchases can undoubtedly be made one of the most effective
means of attracting desirable exhibitors to

future exhibitions, if the question of morality may be waived.

So much has been said about the general influence of exhibitions upon the progress of civilisation, that it seems superfluous to add any remark on that subject here. Institutions that bring into evidence the solidarity of the interests of mankind are the best arguments in favour of universal peace, and International Exhibitions are worthy of every support, because they belong to this class. They make the different nations acquainted with the good qualities of every race, and thus engender feelings of mutual respect. The united efforts of eminent representatives of all countries in the common enterprise, as Commissioners, Jurors and Exhibitors, tend towards abolishing those national antipathies, which are a vestige of former barbarous ages. The courtesy and politeness of manner which cause harmony to reign in these international relations, have fortunately become the characteristic quality of good breeding all over the world; the time has for ever passed when they were a national distinction, as in the days of the Athenians and Bœotians.

We can not better terminate our remarks than in the thoughtful and eloquent words of the philanthropical founder of international exhibitions, the lamented Prince Albert:

"May Divine Providence grant, that the interchange of knowledge resulting from the meeting of enlightened people in friendly rivalry, may be dispersed far and wide over distant lands ; and thus, by showing our mutual dependence upon each other, be a happy means of promoting unity among nations, and peace and good will among the various races of mankind."

POSTSCRIPT.

The foregoing letters were published with the desire to establish the fact, that exhibition matters have arrived at that stage of developement, when it becomes possible to speak of the existence of an exhibition science. An exhibition science with its own peculiar principles, like any other science, cannot fail to bring practice to theoretical consciousness on those points in which the necessity of reform has made itself felt in our past experience.

Exhibitions are a subject particularly adapted for the work of international congresses, for all countries have accepted them, as one of the best means of furthering the intellectual, moral and physical improvement of the population.

In regard to International Exhibitions, an agreement between nations should be their natural foundation. A congress of delegates, appointed by the Ministers of Commerce of the different countries, should be called to study the question, and elaborate a a project for treaty agreements between the different nations in regard to the rules, which are to govern International Exhibitions in future.

One of the first subjects to be considered would be the adoption of a uniform system for the organisation of the Juries, with invariable regulations to direct their work and the distribution of the awards to the exhibitors, between whom in this respect no distinction of nationality should be recognised. — The next important question would be to define the conditions for the participation of foreign countries, and here of course the plan of the distribution of the space is of the highest importance both as regards Universal and Special International Exhibitions. — Lastly, but not least would come the deter-

mination of the order and epochs,
in which such exhibitions are to be
held in the different countries.

The exhibition idea cannot be suc-
cessfully monopolised by any one
country, neither in the form of Universal Exhibitions returning periodi-
cally, nor in that of Special Exhibitions, alternating annually, until they
have embraced the entire domain of
a Universal one. The value of international exhibiting is fully appre-
ciated in all countries, and the question simply resolves itself into this:
will the interests of the trade and
commerce of the world be better served by making International Exhibitions a mutual undertaking of nations,
or by leaving them subject to national
rivalry?

England, the staunch advocate of
the freedom of trade and commerce,
always upholds the principle of recipro-
city as the duty of nations in their
mutual relations. May a hearty coope-
ration of England contribute to make
the next Universal Exhibition, which
it is undoubtedly the turn of Germany

to hold, the occasion of inaugurating
a truly international and cosmopolitan
exhibition policy.

*Dr. Raimund Schramm.**

Geneva, December 1878.

---

*) *Secretary-General and Delegate of the Commission
of Alsace-Lorraine for the Universal Exhibition
of Vienna in 1873.*

*Director of the International Exhibition of the
XX. Congress of German and Austrian Api-
culturists at Strassburg in 1875.*

*Secretary of the Executive Committee of the Grand
Fair in aid of the Wounded within the German
Lines in New York in 1870, etc.*

www.ingramcontent.com/pod-product-compliance
Lightning Source LLC
Chambersburg PA
CBHW021643270326
41931CB00008B/1147